Glory to the Father

A Look at the Mystical Life of Georgette Faniel

DEDICATION AND CONSECRATION

This book is dedicated to Georgette Faniel, whose prayers and extraordinary intercessions have touched my life and the life of my family in so many special ways. It is consecrated to the Most Holy Trinity with the hope that it will truly further the coming of the Kingdom on Earth as it is in Heaven.

Copyright © 1999 St. Andrew's Productions
All Rights Reserved

ISBN: 1-891903-17-9

Published by:

St. Andrew's Productions
6111 Steubenville Pike
McKees Rocks, PA 15136

Tel: (412) 787-9735
Fax: (412) 787-5204

www.SaintAndrew.com

PRINTED IN THE UNITED STATES OF AMERICA

ACKNOWLEDGMENTS

I am indebted to many for assisting and supporting me with this work, especially Frs. Guy and Armand Girard, Georgette Faniel, Robert and Kim Petrisko, Dr. Frank Novasack, Fr. Richard Whetstone - JCOL, Michael Fontecchio, Amanda DeFazio, Carole McElwain, Carol Jean Speck, Joan Smith, Jim Petrilena, Clyde Gualandri, Sister Agnes McCormick, Janice T. Connell, Mary Lou Sokol, and the prayer group at the Pittsburgh Center for Peace.

My loving appreciation to my family; my wife Emily, daughters Maria, Sarah and Natasha, and son, Joshua.

ABOUT THE AUTHOR

D r. Thomas W. Petrisko was the President of the Pittsburgh Center for Peace from 1990 to 1998 and he has served as editor of the Center's six "Queen of Peace" special edition newspapers. These papers were published in many millions throughout the world. He is the author of numerous articles and has written thirteen books on the subject of apparitions, miracles, and supernatural events occuring in the world today: *Call of the Ages, The Sorrow, the Sacrifice and the Triumph, For the Soul of the Family, Mother of the Secret, The Last Crusade, False Prophets of Today, The Prophecy of Daniel, St. Joseph and the Triumph of the Saints, In God's Hands: The Miraculous Story of Little Audrey Santo, The Fatima Prophecies: At the Doorstep of the World, The Kingdom of Our Father, Glory to the Father and The Face of the Father.*

Dr. Petrisko, along with his wife Emily, have three daughters, Maria, Sarah, Natasha, a son, Joshua, and a baby due in August of 1999.

The decree of the Congregation for the Propagation of the Faith (AAS 58, 1186 - approved by Pope Paul VI on 14 October 1966) ruled that the Nihil Obstat and Imprimatur are no longer required for publications that deal with private revelations, apparitions, prophecies, miracles, etc., provided nothing is said in contradiction of faith and morals.

The author hereby affirms his unconditional submission to whatever final judgment is delivered by the Church regarding the events currently under investigation in this book.

FOREWORD

Taste and See the Goodness of the Lord
By Fr. Richard Whetstone, JCOL

I n the beginning, when the Eternal Father created Adam and Eve, we witnessed His great love for us, for He made us in His image and likeness. The profundity is that this loving Father would continually look after all the needs of His creation, looking down from Heaven and beaming because of His love for us.

One day, God did not see His creatures, for there was something in them now, that was not a part of God, and that was sin.

The Eternal Father therefore felt the need to leave His Celestial Court, who continually sing His praise and worship Him in awe, to search for Adam and Eve. This astounded the Celestial Court, for what was the reason for this sudden change? But, God was concerned about us whom He made in His own image and likeness, and so He left Heaven and went to earth and walked in the coolness of the Garden to see where they were.

When God called out to them, by their silence He realized that it was because of their sin. He needed a remedy to get us back into His Kingdom. The solution was to send His beloved Son, to redeem us by His death.

Still we need a constant reminder, and so throughout time, God has given us, through His chosen souls, the witness of His presence with us, so that we might believe and return to Him and His Kingdom. Such it is with the chosen soul Georgette Faniel.

In reading this book, we must read it not with the eyes of the world, for that blinds us in being able to see reality and truth. We must read this book with the eyes of the soul, and in doing so, we are touched by depth and the wisdom that only God can afford us. Reading it with the eyes of the soul, our soul then thirsts for the living waters that God offers. The soul, touched by God, is then drawn like a magnet to His immense love, grace and wisdom.

How wise the hymn, *"Taste and see, the goodness of the Lord."*

I invite you all to, "Taste and see, the goodness of the Lord" through the words, life and the actions of Georgette Faniel.

Very Reverend Richard J. Whetstone, JCOL
May 13, 1999

INTRODUCTION

Now 84 years of age, Canadian mystic and stigmatist Georgette Faniel is recognized worldwide by mystical theologians to be one of the most extraordinary victim souls of the 20th century. Her life reads like a storybook of the miraculous with profound accounts of Heavenly visions and intimate conversations with God. From vivid descriptions of the Celestial Court to wondrous recollections of her conversations with her Heavenly friends, Georgette Faniel's life has been one of great grace and countless blessings.

But most of all, theologians and religious writers have focused on her unparalled revelations of her intimate dialogue with God the Father, the First Person of the Most Holy Trinity. These breathtaking and riveting descriptions of Who the Eternal Father is and how His majestic glory is incomprehensible, have been noted by theologians to be uncanny in their poignant clarity and unique candor. Her 1954 revelation that God the Father told her that **"no church or chapel in the world bears His Name"** left many souls touched and moved to the point that several places of worship are now named after our Heavenly Father.

While perhaps it will not be until after her death that the world will come to completely know her story, *Glory to the Father*, which contains an intimate interview with Georgette Faniel, will allow its readers to begin to grasp the great gift of her life to the Church and to the world. May souls treasure its wisdom and permit its peace and joy to permeate their lives with a deeper love for the awesomeness of our Almighty Father and Creator.

Thomas W. Petrisko
May 13, 1999

PART I

THE MYSTICAL LIFE OF GEORGETTE FANIEL

The history of mystical theology is rich with stories of souls that God chooses to keep hidden from the world in order to better fulfill His mission through them. Many of these souls are in fact never revealed to the public, as God withholds any revelation of their meritorious service on His behalf to Himself and the Church Triumphant. In other cases, we often hear about the lives of chosen ones after their death, sometimes even centuries later, as God carefully engineers the timing of such affairs for the maximum benefit of souls. Finally, there are those hidden servants that God gradually moves from the invisible to the visible while still alive, choosing in His wisdom a blossoming of their life at a certain time and in specific situations that again are carefully designed to aid in the salvation of souls and in the expedition of bringing His Kingdom to reign on earth.

One such chosen instrument is a Canadian woman of Belgian extraction, whose life and revelations indicate that she holds, in God's eyes, great favor, high esteem and perhaps unparalled merit in His service as a hidden victim. Most of all, she has been revealed to be a gem of the Eternal Father, chosen by Him as His instrument to bring peace to the world and spiritual assistance to the Church.

Georgette Faniel was born in 1915 and has resided in Montreal all of her life. As of this writing she is 84 years of age and residing in an elderly home in a suburb of the city. Regarded by many respected theologians as a mystic and victim soul of the highest order, Georgette Faniel's life in God began at the age of six when she first heard the voice of Jesus. However, it was not until 1985, almost seventy years later, that the world began to come to know of her life and special mission.

When Faniel first heard as a child Jesus speak to her, she said the voice resounded in the depth of her heart (inner locution) as well as in her ear (aural locution). This dialogue with Christ became clearer and clearer and she also then began to hear the voice of the Blessed Virgin Mary, the Holy Spirit (not heard as a voice but as an "inner light"), and eventually the Eternal Father. Over time, her heavenly conversations became a normal fact of life and her intimacy with God permitted her to spiritually grow in a way that is comparable to many mystics.

At the beginning of her spiritual experiences, Georgette thought that such divine favors were normal for all children and adults. But when she discovered they were not, she became fearful and withdrawn. Her nights became long episodes of prayer, with only an hour or two devoted to sleep. And like all such chosen souls, the devil would become her nemesis, often ridiculing and tormenting her unmercifully.

Over the years, Georgette's family also added to her cross, as they distanced themselves from her because of her experiences. A Jesuit priest, who believed in her spiritual experiences began to direct and advise her until she finally found a priest who would become her spiritual director. Father Joseph Gamache, S.J., operated in this role for twenty years until he died at the age of 84. After his passing, another Jesuit, Father Paul Mayer, took his place and served as her spiritual director for the next 17 years.

In 1981, Father Mayer asked Georgette to pray for a new spiritual director because of his age. (He was 81 years old.) After a retreat, Georgette says that the Eternal Father instructed her that Fathers Armand and Guy Girard, twins and Canadian priests of the Society of the Holy Apostles of Montreal, were to now assist her. Fr. Armand Girard became her spiritual director while his brother, Father Guy, was to be her spiritual counselor and would have the responsibility of Georgette's spiritual notes. And it was with the advent of the Girard brothers' involvement that Georgette Faniel's life would soon move out from being hidden and into the public realm.

"Like My Son," the Eternal Father told her one day, **"You will have a public life."** At the time, Georgette did not understand the meaning of this revelation nor how it was to come about. For seventy-two years she had remained anonymous and if she had her way, she would refuse to give up her hidden life.

But in October 1984 the Girard brothers made a 10-day pilgrimage/retreat to Medjugorje for the first time and quickly events began to unfold which would reveal the life and mission of Georgette Faniel, especially her intimacy with the Eternal Father.

When the brothers returned to Montreal from Medjugorje, they discussed their spiritual experiences and convictions with Georgette. Her response was tempered, but careful and attentive. She revealed no enthusiasm and advised only prayer.

But on Good Friday of Holy Week in 1985, Georgette Faniel reported that the Eternal Father asked her if she would be willing to give her life in order to authenticate the apparitions in Medjugorje. **"Accept with love,"** the Eternal Father said to Georgette, **"that the testimony on Medjugorje be published so that the apparitions may be made known."** According to her spiritual director, she accepted this request with great faith and joy but knew her sufferings would be worse. Georgette then offered during the Holy Week of 1985 her life as a witness to the authenticity of the apparitions of the Blessed Virgin Mary in Medjugorje.

The following year (October, 1985) the two priests returned to Medjugorje after a seven-day retreat in Rome. There they shared with a Franciscan priest what was occurring with Georgette Faniel in regards to Medjugorje and sought to discern whether or not they were to do more, perhaps in the form of publishing the entire account and sending it to the Holy Father. A message from Mary through the Medjugorje visionary Maria Lunetti encouraged them. Upon returning to Montreal, they requested that Georgette Faniel ask Jesus during the celebration of a Mass in her apartment on November 16, 1985, if the events occurring in Montreal were to be published. **"Why would I have inspired you to offer your life to bear witness to the authenticity of the apparitions of the Blessed Virgin at Medjugorje?"** the Eternal Father responded with authority. With this confirmation, the two priests set about to write the book, *Mary Queen of Peace Stay with Us*. It was an account of testimonies in favor of Medjugorje, especially Georgette Faniel's words and mystical experiences in regards to the apparitions there.

The Girard brothers wrote their account with the interest that its contents were to remain confidential; only to be seen by two priests in Medjugorje. But the priests there, after having it translated into Croatian and reviewed by a few persons, wrote back to the Girard brothers that it seemed Georgette Faniel should not remain hidden anymore and the book needed to be published. When put in question by Georgette to the Father on whether or not the book, which contained so much about herself be published, the Father replied, **"Why should I have kept you in warm soil for years, if not so that you may produce much fruit?"** Faniel (now 71 years old) protested, "If the seed does not die in the soil it

8

cannot bear fruit." To which the Father replied, **"I agree, but I want you to die to your own will."** He added **"I have already told you; like My Son, you are to have a public life."** The Eternal Father also told Georgette Faniel why this was necessary:

> **Through the total gift of your life, you are the treasure of the Church where the lowly, the poor, the sick, of the Church, all of mankind will go to acquire riches in face of our espousals. You are the beloved daughter of the Virgin Mary, Queen of Peace, and you are the gem of the Holy Trinity. By accepting Our will, you live with your beloved spouse the total gift of yourself as priest and victim, to glorify Me and to sustain the Holy Father, the consecrated souls and humanity. Accept with love that this testimony be published to make known the authenticity of the apparitions. Renounce your own will to accept only Our holy and adorable will on you. This act of surrender is the sublime act of your life as spouse of Christ, as mother of your spiritual children, as handmaid of the Blessed Trinity and as confidante of the Virgin Mary, Queen of Peace.**
>
> **We thank you and keep this peace of heart, soul and mind. The most beautiful gift you can offer Us is to surrender your will. You are living at this moment the beautiful prayer of the complete gift of yourself. Commend your will into My hands as My Son did on the cross through love. You must die as a victim of our love for the Church and for mankind which I have entrusted to you. Remain faithful to Us to the end, then it will be the beginning of a new life with Us for eternity.**

Indeed, the purpose of the Girard brothers' book can now be seen to have transcended its original intent–it shines a bright light on the face of the Father through the life of

Georgette Faniel. Faniel's testimony in the book profoundly reveals our wonderful and omnipotent heavenly Father by offering the reader a glimpse of His intimate presence within all souls, and how, through chosen souls like Faniel, He desires that all souls come to love, honor, and serve Him in a special way.

The book especially reveals how the Eternal Father has come to embrace His servant Georgette Faniel in a special way through a series of mystical phenomena. On Georgette's body a mark in the shape of the number two was revealed in her flesh (lower abdomen). This mark, the Father told her, was to signify her "alliance" with God in the flesh. Received on the Feast of the Precious Blood in 1982, Georgette heard Jesus then say to her **"Now we are two in one same flesh."** Medical doctors have marveled at this mystical phenomenon. Doctor Alain Farley examined it and described what he saw and thought: "As a doctor, I have never seen a sign like this. It is unbelievable. This sign looks like a luminous neon whereby we can see the blood circulating, blood that is perfectly synthesized with the beating of the heart, and yet it is not like with any adjacent organ or blood vessels. I see it very well even if the number two is very small."

Another doctor took a photo of the mark with a hospital camera. The camera was equipped with a magnifying lens. The doctor had to take this photo while kneeling, therefore he obtained a perfect photo. Why did he have to kneel? According to Father Guy Girard, it was God who made it so that to see the miracle "one must kneel as a sign of a respect to the meaning of the sign." The number "2" on Georgette's body is made up of seven red dots depicting, the priest say, the seven gifts of the Holy Spirit. Several months after its appearance, Jesus said to Georgette, **"You must call this: 'the Alliance.'**

A second mystical phenomenon that Georgette experiences is known as the transfixion or transverberation. This is an experience that causes her to feel a sensation "like a burning arrow of fire piercing her heart." The pain is extremely intense and increases when this arrow or "dart" is drawn out. Saint Teresa of Avilla and St. John of the Cross have given a description of the transfixion. Said St. John of the Cross concerning this mystical gift, "Lord, wound me with a wound of love which may be healed only by being wounded again." When asked to describe the transfixion Georgette says, "I feel my soul must never cease giving thanks while Jesus is wounding my heart. I thank him for this suffering and I offer it to Him. At that moment, there is very great interior joy in my soul. The greatest joy of the world cannot compare with what I feel within myself."

According to Father Guy Girard, the Eternal Father asks Georgette to offer these sufferings for the needs of the Church and for the world. But very often, the Eternal Father asked her to offer these wounds for specific persons, such as the Holy Father, for the consecrated souls, for priests, for bishops, for those who need prayers and for visionaries in order that they will be protected from their enemies, visible and invisible.

Some of Georgette's suffering have been especially extraordinary, such as the time she offered to suffer for a young girl who was pregnant and wished to get an abortion. After meeting with Georgette and Georgette offering to accept her sufferings, the young woman experienced a flawless and painless pregnancy and delivery. Meanwhile, Georgette's abdomen gradually swelled over the nine months and she endured the pain of the delivery. A similar story is revealed by her spiritual director who complained of a swollen and painful knee that made it difficult to climb the steps of Georgette's apartment. Georgette apparently interceded on his behalf, unbeknownst to him after he disclosed his affliction. Upon his return the next day, his knee was fine. But when he met with Georgette, one of her knees was swollen and apparently painful, although she said nothing of the matter.

But most of all it is Georgette Faniel's relationship with

the Eternal Father that emerged from the Girard brother's book. As a child, Faniel says she heard the voice of Mary and Jesus, but it was not until much later in her life that she heard the voice of the Eternal Father. It was Mary, she says, that led her to the Father and taught her how to accept the Father's will on all occasions.

Through Mary, Georgette learned of the Father's love and mercy and came to understand His boundless tenderness and infinite patience, attributes that He wants all His children to know He possesses for them in His Heart. "It is while contemplating the wounds of Jesus," says Faniel, "that I grasped the infinite love of the Father for each one of us, especially for the most abject, among whom I belong."

Georgette Faniel came to the devotion of the Eternal Father by listening to Him attentively: "I could see His great mercy in my life and so I began to know Him better and to serve and love Him better. This is the purpose of our life on earth. One revelation concerning the Eternal Father through Georgette Faniel has especially been noted and has brought a response from around the world. In her spiritual notes, the Eternal Father, said to her in 1954, **"There is no chapel or church dedicated to Me in the whole world."** This revelation has led to chapels being constructed or rededicated in the Father's name throughout the world. Likewise, some now seek to discern the building of a great shrine in honor of God our Father, so that He may be better known and loved as our Creator, our Father, Who is filled with love for all His children.

While Georgette Faniel still lives today a life of prayer, she says she especially prays for the "arrival" of the Father's Kingdom; for His peace to reign on earth and for all His children to come to love, honor, and serve Him in a special way:

"I pray that the Kingdom of God come.
That it arrive. It is difficult for me to say "Thy

Kingdom come." I prefer "Thy Kingdom arrive." To come seems so far off. If I say: "our friends are coming," even if it brings joy, it seems remote. But when I say: "They are arriving" I am more joyful. I pray that God change our hearts, that He purify our hearts by the Precious Blood of Jesus. I pray that the Precious Blood of Jesus be as powerful now as it ever was, I pray that God the Father be known and loved as our Creator, our Father who is filled with love for all His children. I pray that we speak to others about Him, that the whole world might have the same privilege of knowing the God that we have. Believers or nonbelievers, we were all created by the Father's hands and we will all stand before Him one day. Most of us tend to forget that basic truth."

PART II

AN INTERVIEW WITH GEORGETTE FANIEL

The following interview with Georgette Faniel gives us an intimate look at the mystical life of this chosen soul and how God Our Father is speaking to her, is really speaking to all mankind.

THE EARLY YEARS

Q. - *Tell me, what were the first graces you received in your life?*

A. - At about the age of six I began to hear the voice of Jesus in my heart. I thought that this constant dialogue with Jesus was normal for all children.

Q. - *You must have been happy to hear that voice!*

A. - Yes, but I have often wished not to hear the voice of Jesus anymore, for to remain faithful to our Lord's requests is very demanding. Moreover, Satan would tell me that this was all fake (sheer invention)!

Q. - *Did you speak of this to anyone?*

A. - No, because I was afraid of being ridiculed and my soul as a child was often in anguish. At that time, Satan used to tell me that I was damned. He would tell me: "You have made a bad confession... You have committed a sacrilege." I was torn and I often wept at the thought of having lost my Blessed Jesus and my friendship with the Virgin Mary. Nevertheless, I always took refuge in her. It was only later that my soul as a child was enlightened.

Q. - *You have, therefore, spoken much to Jesus!*

A. - Not only with Jesus, but also with the Father and the Holy Spirit and with the Most Blessed Virgin Mary as well.

Q. - *You mean to say that you also hear the voice of the EternalFather, the voice of the Holy Spirit...the voice of Mary.*

A. - Yes, that is so...

Q. - *But how can you tell them apart?*

A. - The voice of the Divine Persons is sensed in the innermost depths of my heart, and also in my ear...

Q. - *How do they address you?*

A. - They communicate with me in different words and expression. The tone of the voice is also different.

Q. - *How does the Eternal Father speak to you?*

A. - He speaks with more authority, but also with great love and great mercy. His voice is more solemn. I feel that a certain reverent but loving awe invades my heart, as the Father speaks to His child.

Q. - *Can you speak in this sense about Jesus as well?*

A. - Jesus addresses me in a more personal language. He calls me: **"My Beloved, My little Bride...My little host of love, My little victim of love."** His language is one of gentleness and if He chides me, He consoles me at the same time for the grief I feel.

Q. - *What does He tell you?*

A. - Jesus asks me to accept great sufferings and to unite these sufferings to His Passion. He asks me to follow Him, to accept the will of the Eternal Father in all things, no matter the circumstance and to never ask, "Why?"

Q. - *And the Holy Spirit?*

A. - He especially helps me in the decision I have to make. I feel deep within me that it is the Holy Spirit who directs my prayer. He helps me in everything, even in material tasks.

Q. - *Do you understand very well that the Persons of the Trinity are distinct?*

A. - Yes, I see it within me with a kind of evidence but

I do not have the words to explain it. I also see that they make but one God.

Q. - *You have told me that the Virgin Mary spoke to you. What role does she play in your life?*

A. - She is my Mother! I am her daughter. She is part of my intimacy with God.

Q. - *What does she talk about to you?*

A. - She speaks to me of the mercy of the Father towards mankind. She speaks to me of her Son Jesus, of all He has suffered for me. She tells me to be very attentive to the graces of the Holy Spirit and to His inspirations. She is my confidante. She directs me to the Cross of her Son as she shows me how to conform myself totally to the will of the Father.

Q. - *Does she do anything else for you?*

A. - Yes, Mary is the one who guides me in my spiritual life. She is the one who gives me formative training.

Q. - *What do you mean by formative training?*

A. - She teaches me how to understand what God accomplishes in me. She teaches me humility; it is always with an infinite tact and a motherly gentleness that she admonishes me when I do not amend my failings.

Q. - *Georgette, now I see how the three Divine Persons*

and the Virgin Mary have led you. Is there a priest who has guided you in your spiritual life?

A. - I waited for almost twenty years before I found a priest, a spiritual director, who would find out about my life and have grace to believe in it.

Q. - *Who was this priest?*

A. - Father Joseph Gamache, S.J., was my spiritual director for twenty (20) years. He passed away at the age of eighty-four (84).

Q. - *And after his death?*

A. - Father Paul Mayer, S.J., was my second spiritual director. He directed me for 17 years. He was the one who asked me to pray so that the Eternal Father would clearly show me the one who should be my new spiritual director. He asked me to make a retreat for that purpose....

Q. - *When did you find out?*

A. - I did not want to choose one according to my personal inclinations. I prayed very much and on December 8, 1983, on the Feast of the Immaculate Conception, during the celebration of the Holy Mass, I clearly heard the Virgin Mary indicating the very specific choice of the Eternal Father. **"Father Armand will be your spiritual director and Father Guy Girard will be your spiritualcounselor and will be responsible for your spiritual notes."**

Q. - *Georgette, do you believe that other people can hear this inner voice?*

A. - Yes, I am convinced of that. I am not a person specifically set aside. We must be attentive to the inspirations of grace which we receive in prayer, and in silence be constantly asking the Blessed Virgin to lead us to the Father with Jesus. We must not seek the marvelous. It is in the simplicity of the heart, the soul and the spirit that God manifests Himself. We must humbly ask the Virgin Mary to teach us how to love and serve the Father. The soul which asks with faith and sincerity is always answered. Never does the Father reject a prayer! He chooses His hour! We must be ready to wait.

Q. - *Obviously, prayer is the road we must travel to reach intimacy with the divine. Georgette, you have journeyed through this spiritual ascent which has not yet come to an end. When you were young, how did you pray?*

A. - One of the first incidents which challenged me was the following one. When I injured myself at the age of four, my grandmother asked me to unite my suffering to that of Jesus. She would say: "Look at Jesus. He has not only one finger which is hurting but his whole hand." I would kiss the crucifix and say to my grandmother: "This hurts just the same!" Meanwhile, I always grew up with this inner voice speaking to me. It was something absolutely normal for me. I did not attach any importance to it. I liked to go and pray in solitude and quiet. It was then that the dialogue with Jesus was more intimate.

Q. - *How much time did you devote to prayer?*

A. - Prayer was my refuge in joy as in grief. I would ask the Eternal Father to protect me. I would devote as much time as possible to it. When I was about 15, I would make at least one holy hour each day.

Q. - *Don't you believe that the length of time you devoted to prayers was exaggerated?*

A. - No, I didn't think so. To give one out of 24 hours is not exaggerated. God takes care of us 24 hours a day.

Q. - *Were there other means that helped you in your spiritual journey?*

A. - Yes, I had consecrated myself to Mary in the Congregation of the Children of Mary.

Q. - *Something else, possibly?*

A. - Yes, at 17, I offered myself as a victim to the Merciful Love for the salvation of the world. This was a group called: "The Association of Victim Souls" for which Father Charette, a Dominican, was responsible.

Q. - *Did you make any vows?*

A. - Yes, I made the three vows (poverty, chastity, obedience) in the presence of my spiritual director, Father Gamache, S.J.

Q. - *Did you then make any other vows?*

A. - Yes, my director asked me if I was willing to make the vow of immolation and offer myself as a sacrifice of love to the Eternal Father for the consecrated souls. This I did with joy. Later Jesus spoke to me of a spiritual betrothal.

Q. - *Can you tell us when Jesus first spoke to you?*

A. - Shortly after my first communion, Jesus manifested Himself to me as a friend and companion, asking me to be united to Him constantly through prayer and through the Holy Eucharist. It's what I've endeavored to do throughout my whole life.

Q. - *Has Jesus appeared to you?*

A. - Not visibly. From time to time I see Him as a silhouette.

Q. - *Can you describe Jesus to us?*

A. - He is all good and all compassion. He is mindful of every human being on earth.

Q. - *Did you know what this meant?*

A. - I understood it from what Jesus was telling me. But I always knew myself to be unworthy. It seemed to me that this was only for consecrated men and women.

Q. - *When did Jesus ask you to become His Betrothed?*

A. - On February 22, 1953. " **I want you as my betrothed,**" He said to me. "**And you will wear**

the ring that your spiritual director will bless. This ring will always protect you. It will help you to fulfill your role as the betrothed of Christ an to be faithful to it. You, you are nothing. As for Me, I am everything."

Q. - *Was this commitment demanding for you?*

A. - Yes, a greater demand for prayer in order to respond to what God expects of me. But, I had moments of rebellion when I removed my ring and threw it away for I did not want to have anything to do with Jesus's demands anymore.

Q. - *What was Jesus's reaction?*

A. - Jesus was hurt by this vile gesture of revolt. His heart was wounded because of all that He had done for me. He would tell me: **"With what love I leaned over you when you were wounded by sin!"** Jesus then leaned over me with much more love and care.

Q. - *How did you live after that period of revolt?*

A. - It was a period of aridity, struggles, attacks from Satan who wanted to destroy me. "You have no reason to keep on living," Satan would tell me. I felt no more attraction for prayer. Even the Sacraments had become a burden for me. My spiritual director wearied me. It seemed to me that he had become an obstacle to my spiritual life.

Q. - *And then?*

A. - Then, my spiritual director compelled me to write all

that I was experiencing in order to check more closely my spiritual life and all that my hidden intimacy contained. This was painful to me for I felt I was betraying a secret which I had shared with Jesus and Mary ever since my childhood. These were difficult moments. This hidden intimacy was known to no one then. I experienced a feeling of betrayal. I felt guilty even when I spoke of this to my spiritual director. But one day, the Lord told me: **"Tell him everything, he represents Me."** I did not believe that suffering united to that of Jesus had the dimension of redemption and purification. I perceived suffering as a punishment.

Q. - *How did you perceive God?*

A. - I felt He was remote. I did not want to see a crucifix anymore. His wounds turned me away from Him. In the state of soul I was in, I did not believe anymore that this was purification. I did not believe what Father Gamache, my spiritual director, told me anymore. One day, this priest said: "Your soul cost the Blood of Christ and it is costing me as well." It was only later that I understood what that priest had done in prayer, self-denial, fasting to help me and to liberate my soul. He was the one who made me respond to what God was expecting of me.

Q. - *After this spiritual journey, what did God ask you to do?*

A. - He asked me to sever myself from my family, my surroundings, my friends and He led me to renounce my will. This was the most important: to sever myself

24

from myself.

Q. · *What does all this self-denial represent for you?*

A. · It makes me realize that without God I can do nothing. It makes me understand His infinite mercy, for I can see Him, His arms stretched out towards us to receive us whatever be the state of our souls. I see Him blind to our sins, our failings, His heart full of love always ready to accept us. All He asks of a soul is good will, sincerity, trust in His infinite mercy for each one of us. What is most important is conformity to the will of the Father in all things and in all places, as Jesus and Mary achieved it!

SUFFERING IN CHRIST

Q. · *How do you understand the vow as priest and victim which you made some time ago?*

A. · This vow is the culminating point of all my life. I recall that since the age of four, I have always felt suffering in my body. From this day onward, Jesus is inviting me to identify myself with Him as priest and victim in the perfect and full development of royal priesthood. Jesus made me grasp the fact that Holy Mass is not primarily a meal, but that it is the ultimate sacrifice of Jesus dying on the cross for the salvation of the world. At the moment of the consecration, I unite myself to the sacrificial Lamb. The Eucharist is the source of my strength.

Q. · *Tell me something about the wounds of Jesus*

hidden in your body. Since when do you have them?

A. - In 1950, Jesus made me understand that I had His most holy wounds.

Q. - *Do you have the wounds of Jesus's hands and feet?*

A. - Yes, I have them. The Father gave them to me as a pure gift and I feel very unworthy of having them.

Q. - *Precisely, where is the pain of the hands of Jesus located?*

A. - The nails to support the body of Jesus on the cross were driven through the wrists. This is where the pains are the most acute and the most intense.

Q. - *And the feet?*

A. - No, it is a little different for the feet. When I am lying down, I always have my feet one on top of the other.

Q. - *Where are the wounds in the feet?*

A. - They are on the side, the left foot supports the right foot. When the Lord asks for much suffering, He is the One who places my feet.

Q. - *And the crown of thorns?*

A. - I received it on April 25, 1953. Jesus told me on that day: **'Today I am setting My crown of thorns on your head.'**

Q. - *Did you have difficulty in accepting it?*

A. · No, I am not worthy of it, but I accepted that the will of God be done.

Q. · *Is it always more or less painful?*

A. · It is much more painful on Fridays for two reasons: because it is the day of the Lord's death, and the other reason depends on what Jesus demands.

Q. · *Did the medical doctors try to find where the pains come from?*

A. · Yes, but the doctors found nothing! When the Lord chooses a victim for Himself, neither the doctors nor science can find the source and the intensity of the pains to nurse them. Jesus told me: **'It is only after your death that doctors will be able to know the pains that you have borne.'**

Q. · *What about the wound of the pierced heart of Jesus?*

A. · The wound of the heart of Jesus is a persistent pain which never stops, but the wound on the shoulder is the most painful.

Q. · *People never speak of that wound on the shoulder.*

A. · I know but, precisely, this sixth wound that Jesus has, is very painful. Jesus is the one Who showed me that the wound of the shoulder was the most painful of all during the carrying of the cross. It was after considerable research that my spiritual director, Father Joseph Gamache, S.J., discovered that the existence of the sixth wound located on the shoulder had been revealed to Saint Bernard:

'While carrying the cross I had a wound three fingers deep and three bones were laid bare on My shoulder.'

Q. - *Did you ask on which shoulder was this wound?*

A. - Yes, I asked Jesus and He told me: **"I was carrying the cross on My left shoulder (on the side of My heart) in order to keep My right hand free to bless My people a last time."**

Q. - *Would you add anything else to these answers?*

A. - Yes, I would say that the interior sufferings of Jesus were greater than His physical sufferings: **'My soul is sad unto death,'** He sighed. He was experiencing the agony of the soul, the heart and the spirit. The heart of Jesus was wounded by the ingratitude of men. Jesus died of having loved too much! His heart was opened by love even before the soldier pierced it to check if He was dead. This was but a symbolic gesture.

Q. - *Georgette, you have already spoken to me about a mark made by God on your body. Could you tell me something more about this manifestation of God towards you?*

A. - Yes, on February 2, 1982, on the Feast of the Purification, the Lord asked me to offer more suffering for the Holy Father, for the consecrated souls, and to accept to bear the sins of mankind.

Q. - *What happened then?*

A. - I agreed to everything, but I had only the usual suffering. I found myself and always find myself unworthy of bearing the sins of mankind when I am a sinner myself.

Q. - *And then?*

A. - On Good Friday, 1982, I had much more suffering. It was in these great pains that God was manifesting Himself. ThroughHis grace, I understood the importance of what God has demanded of me on February 2, 1982.

Q. - *Then?*

A. - On the Feast of the Precious Blood, God manifestedHimself for the third time by renewing His request.

Q. - *How? By words or by signs?*

A. - God was manifesting His request by a sharp pain on the right side and by leaving a mark in my flesh in the shape of this number two. As I looked, I saw a red spot in the shape of a two in which blood was circulating normally.

Q. - *Did you speak of this manifestation of God to your spiritual director?*

A. - Yes, I confided to Him what was happening to me.

Q. - *And your director?*

A. - Then my director asked me if I knew the meaning of what was happening to me. As I was saying no for the second time, Jesus intervened: **You will answer your director: Now we are two in one same flesh.**

Q. - *Did you say that to your director?*

A. - Yes, I had to say it.

Q. - *And he?*

A. - Then my director replied: "If that is so, you have not come to the end of your suffering!" And he added: "Thank the Lord, you have received a great favor."

Q. - *After that, was there greater suffering?*

A. - Yes, greater suffering was felt on the right side, but only when there was a very specific reason.

Q. - *Did your director demand a proof of this manifestation?*

A. - Yes, he asked me to have it checked by a physician and to have a photo taken of it.

Q. - *Did the doctor do the checking as had been requested?*

A. - Yes, the doctor checked it. He had to kneel to see it better. Jesus was making me know that the doctor had to kneel to see the sign of God inlaid in my flesh. Fearing that this was my imagination at work, I did not dare ask him to kneel down. Then I asked Jesus to inspire him to kneel down. At the moment I was asking him, he knelt and saw the shape of the two perfectly.

Q. - *What was his reaction?*

A. - He was amazed when he examined it with a magnifying glass while telling me: "As a doctor, I have never seen a sign like this. It is unbelievable; this sign looks like a luminous neon where we can see the blood circulating, blood that is perfectly synchronized with the beating of the heart, and yet is not linked with any adjacent organ. I see it very well even if the number is very small.

Q. - *Was a photo taken as requested by your spiritual director?*

A. - Yes, photos were taken, but without any results. When I spoke to my director, he said: "I am asking you to try one last time. If the photo is not a success, this is an indication that God does not wish this sign impressed in your flesh to be seen. This is, therefore, the last authorization I am giving you."

Q. - *Did the last photo give any results?*

A. - Yes, the photo was taken by another doctor who used the hospital camera. This camera was equipped with a magnifying lens. This photo was a perfect success, but this doctor also had to take it while kneeling.

Q. - *Why must they kneel to take this photo?*

A. - Out of respect for the meaning of this sign: TWO IN ONE SAME FLESH.

Q. - *What did the photo reveal?*

A. - It clearly revealed the presence of blood in the number two. This number is made up of seven red dots.

Q. - *What is the meaning of the seven red dots?*

A. - They mean the Seven Gifts of the Holy Spirit. Now that several months have gone by, Jesus told me: **'Henceforth, the number two must be called the ALLIANCE.'**

Q. - *Why did Jesus want it so?*

A. - Because the ALLIANCE shows the intimacy of God with the soul and it also means a greater identification with suffering of the crucified Christ. We will never be able to imagine the extent to which God loves us.

Q. - *Tell us more about the Alliance.*

A. - That is very difficult for me to do. Do you want me to mention everything about it?

Q. - *Please.*

A. - One day I felt a sharp pain on my right side. As I had recently had my gall bladder removed, I thought the pain was coming from the incision where the drain had been. When I looked, I saw the number two perfectly produced by seven small blood spots. Blood circulates freely in each of these spots but there are no organs there and therefore no reason for that blood to circulate. I asked the lady who was living with me to have a look and to tell me what she saw. She said: "That's odd! The doctors wrote the number two on your side. Are you going to have a second operation?" I said "no". The following day, the Lord told me: "**We are two in one flesh and I want to mark our Alliance in your flesh.**" My dedication to this Alliance is twofold: first, fidelity and second the offering of my suffering, united to Jesus' Passion. It has been with me for the last twelve years. When someone is allowed to witness the Alliance, that person is asked to pray: "My Lord and my God, I believe, I adore your Presence in their Alliance. By the Precious Blood of Jesus your Son, I exalt Thee in union with Mary, our Heavenly Mother." The Lord also told me that this Alliance would be my shield against all enemies, visible and invisible.

Q. - *The 1st of July is the Feast of the Precious Blood.*

A. - Yes, and Jesus showed me that the suffering I bear must identify me with Christ, priest and victim, to help the Holy Father, the consecrated souls, the Church and all of mankind.

Q. - *Did you ask Jesus any other questions about the ALLIANCE?*

A. - Jesus made me understand not to ask any questions out of sheer curiosity. But he told me that this grace of the ALLIANCE is unique in the world.

Q. - *Georgette, one day, during the celebration of the Eucharist, at the moment you received the Precious Blood of Christ, I saw your face full of suffering and your hands were clasped over your heart. What was going on?*

A. - I had a sharp pain in my heart.

Q. - *Does this happen often?*

A. - Yes, it often happens during the day, sometimes during the night and also while I am working.

Q. - *What is this pain like?*

A. - It is like a deep wound.

Q. - *Can you describe this wound to me?*

A. - It is like a burning arrow of fire piercing my heart. The pain is extremely intense and increases when this arrow or dart is drawn out.

Q. - *What happens then?*

A. - I feel my soul must never cease giving thanks while Jesus is wounding my heart. I thank Him for this suffering and I offer it to Him. At that moment, there is a very great interior joy in my soul. The greatest joys of the world cannot compare with what I feel within myself.

Q. - *For whom do you offer this suffering?*

A. - I constantly offer this indescribable suffering to the Father in union with Jesus and Mary for the Holy Father, for the consecrated souls and for the whole Church.

Q. - *Do you wish to have that wound?*

A. - Yes, I want it but I do not ask for it. I want to protect myself from all self-seeking. Jesus knows that in the innermost depths of myself, I want it. This wound makes me more like Jesus crucified.

Q. - *How is that? Why does it make you more like Jesus crucified?*

A. - Because I unite my will to that of the Father as Jesus did all His life, but especially on the cross.

Q. - *Are there any moments when these wounds are more painful and cause greater suffering?*

A. - On Fridays, and when God the Father asks for more suffering for the needs of the Church.

Q. - *Does the Father ask you to offer these wounds for specific persons?*

A. - Yes, for the Holy Father, for the consecrated souls, for the priests of Medjugorje, for the boys and girls who see the Blessed Virgin, so that they will be protected from their enemies, visible and invisible, for the bishops of Yugoslavia, as well as for all those who recommend themselves to our prayers.

Q. - *Does the Eternal Father ask for prayers for the apparitions of Medjugorje every day?*

A. - Yes, and I assume it upon myself as a duty. Since I heard of Medjugorje, I pray and offer my suffering so that the authenticity of the apparitions may be recognized as quickly as possible.

Q. - *Do you offer these wounds of the heart for any other intentions?*

A. - Yes, I offer them so that the message of Mary, Queen of Peace, may be spread in all its authenticity throughout the whole world. Mary's message brings peace to souls and does not trouble them. The Most Blessed Virgin Mary never troubles souls. She always wants to lead them to the heart of Jesus and to the heart of the Father.

Q. - *Does the Stigmata still cause you pain?*

A. - Constantly. But I suffer from them more on Good Friday and on other special occasions. I offer it all to the Lord and I thank Him for it.

Q. - *Are these wounds primarily a grace for yourself?*

A. - Yes, a very great grace! But we must not forget that Jesus has given His most holy wounds to the world, and that it is by these wounds that we are healed. As for myself, I share these wounds of the heart with the souls God entrusts to me especially those of the priest and the consecrated.

Q. - *Do you know the prayer of Saint John of the Cross concerning these wounds of the heart?*

A. - No, but I would like to know it to recite it.

Q. - *It is most beautiful! Here it is: "Lord, wound me with a wound of love which may be healed only by being wounded again."*

A. - Thank you. Saint John of the Cross expressed this very well. From now on, I will be able to recite it.

MYSTICAL FAVORS AND CROSSES

Q. - *Georgette, have you ever been favored with visions?*

A. - I have occasionally had inner visions but these moments of my life have always brought me very great suffering.

Q. - *Since you have heard about Medjugorje, have you had inner visions of the Virgin Mary concerning these apparitions?*

A. - Yes. I saw her in an inner vision. I saw her weeping because of her priests, her favorite sons. That is beyond description. It is like an image which imprints itself in my soul. It can never be forgotten.

Q. - *Can you tell us when Mary first spoke to you?*

A. - Mary first spoke to me when I was six years old, just before my first communion, in order to prepare my heart to receive Jesus.

Q. - *Did she ever appear to you?*

37

A. - Yes, many times.

Q. - *Can you describe Mary for us?*

A. - One cannot describe her beauty. Everything about her touches my heart and my soul.

Q. - *How does the Queen of Peace reveal herself to you?*

A. - To me, the Queen of Peace reveals herself nearer and nearer to me. Mary is the INVISIBLE PRESENCE to the world to give peace and the Holy Father John Paul II is the VISIBLE PRESENCE to ask for that Peace. It is through the apparitions of the Virgin Mary that the message of peace is brought to the earth. This message of peace will be carried throughout the world by the messenger of peace who is the Holy Father John Paul II.

Q. - *What does she ask of you?*

A. - Mary asks me to serve her Son, to accept the will of the Father in my life and to spread the messages of Medjugorje.

Q. - *Since you have heard about Medjugorje, have you had inner visions of the Virgin Mary concerning these apparitions?*

A. - Yes, one day after I had prayed that these apparitions might be recognized and that the obstacles might disappear, I saw the Virgin Mary weeping.

Q. - *What did you feel?*

A. - I felt grief. I was convinced that she was weeping because of the situation at Medjugorje.

Q. - *Can one imagine hearing her weep?*

A. - It is not imagination. When I hear her weeping because of her consecrated souls, her tears are sobs, they are like a physical pain.

Q. - *Is it the same in the case of Medjugorje?*

A. - No, in the case of Medjugorje, I did not hear sobs as it were. She was weeping profusely, but in the silence and the dignity of a mother and of a Queen.

Q. - *Can you explain to me the content of the visions which are linked with Medjugorje?*

A. - In these visions, I see the Virgin Mary. She is earnestly asking for prayers for the priests of Medjugorje, but also for the priests who visit this holy place, for the pilgrims and the visionaries, so that they may remain faithful to what the Virgin Mary asks of them.

Q. - *Are there other requests?*

A. - Yes, at the time of these visions, one request of the Virgin Mary is very explicit and is made with much insistence. She asks to pray so that the Church may recognize, through the power of the Holy Spirit, the authenticity of the apparitions for the glory of the Father and that of Jesus.

Q. -   *What is your relationship to Mary now?*

A. -   It's difficult to answer such a question as it implies
many private and intimate matters. Mary speaks to
me as a mother speaks to her daughter. I
continuously seek refuge in her motherly arms where
she protects me and loves me with the love of the
Father, the Son, and the Holy Spirit. Our Lady loves
me in my weaknesses, my miseries. I feel secure by
her side. Mary accepted Jesus words at the foot of the
Cross and I know that she intercedes for each and
everyone of us when we pray with faith and
confidence , as a child who runs to his mother when
he is hurt. When someone comes to me for prayers,
I place that person into Our Lady's care because I
know how she will pray to the Father for that person
and that the Father cannot say "No" to Mary because
Mary always answered "yes" to the will of the Father
as did Jesus. It is by faith that I believe Mary to be
Mediatrix of all Graces. She intercedes for each and
every one of us even during times of war all over the
world. God calls us and sends us all kind of signs but
people don't understand. We watch television and
witness these wars, famines, earthquakes. News
reports are so depressing that many don't want to
watch them anymore. These reports leave us feeling
helpless against calamities of such magnitude. It is
only through prayer that we can have a different
vision of world events and those of us whom divine
providence spares from such a fate must pray with all
our hearts in communion with our brothers and
sisters through the holy Sacraments. We must offer
our prayers and our lives for those lands of
martyrdom that suffer from the rages of war.

The Girard brothers book that features Georgette Faniel.

Georgette Faniel at her home in Montreal

**Father Armand Girard, Georgette Faniel,
Father Guy Girard, Pentecost, 1982.**

**In this beautiful 'Chapel of the Eternal Father' rise prayers
of offering for the "Triumph of Mary."
This chapel is located at Cité de la Santé' Hospital, Laval.**

Visitors from the Pittsburgh Center for Peace
on a visitation with Georgette Faniel in Montreal

Fr. Guy Girard, Georgette's spiritual advisor,
with the author, Thomas Petrisko

MARY, QUEEN OF PEACE, STAY WITH US

Look at this picture. It is you there,
with Jesus in the Virgin Mary's arms.
She is your Mother! It is the Eternal
Father who has given Her to you.
Never can He forget you. She has
loved and accepted you at the foot of
the Holy Cross. "Here is your
Mother," she will always protect you.
Thank you for being the Mother of
Jesus and my Mother.

This picture and its message were inspired
and arranged by Georgette Faniel.

To order copies please call: (412) 787-9735

Georgette Faniel with Maria and Sarah Petrisko (1994).

Georgette Faniel with Alvie Keene (L)
and Sister Agnes McCormick (R).

46

Q. - *Have you anything else to add to what you have just told me?*

A. - Yes. Mary's requests involve the fidelity of the villagers to prayer, to the eucharist, to fasting, to the rosary, and to theSacrament of Reconciliation. This fidelity can only promote a greater fidelity to Mary's requests among the pilgrims.

Q. - *Did you have other visions?*

A. - I saw the Holy Father John Paul II experience a very great loneliness. I remember the day of his election when he was telling the world: "Do not be afraid!" A woman I was with said: "This Polish Pope, young and exceptionally healthy, will live a long time." But I distinctly heard in my heart and in my ear: **"He is young, but men will make a prematurely aged man of him."**

Q. - *What is the content of the other visions?*

A. - It is about the Holy Father John Paul II. The Virgin Mary wants me understand to pray more for him because of the great responsibility he bears: that of leading the people of God to the Father.

Q. - *Do the inner visions have other purposes?*

A. - Yes, through these visions, the Virgin Mary is asking me to pray for certain events which are happening in the world. She is also asking me to pray for people who are victims of natural disasters, or the wickedness of men, injustice, or violence. All these

47

evils are rooted in pride. We must humbly ask the Eternal Father to change our hearts by a greater love for God and of our neighbor. This intercession must always be made in the faith and trust that our prayer can be answered.

Q. - *Have you ever bilocated?*

A. - I am not aware of it. Some people have mentioned seeing me in different places while I haven't been out of my home in years except to go to the hospital.

Q. - *Georgette, I notice that people are very eager to see you. Why?*

A. - They come for advice or for help.

Q. - *Do you welcome them willingly?*

A. - Yes, Jesus told me: "**Welcome all the people whom I will send to you. Greet them as if they were Myself.**"

Q. - *You tell me you help them. In what way?*

A. - The Holy Spirit inspires me only when I am in the presence of the person; I begin to relate a fact in which the person concerned recognized himself. What God wants me to describe is often a situation identical to the problem presented.

Q. - *Can we say that you have the power of reading souls?*

A. - No. The Holy Spirit does not reveal the state of souls to me. However, He can give me a feeling of the state of a soul, that is, of grief, anxiety, fear, worry. All that stems from the lack of faith, of surrender to the Father's will. God can also allow these states to be a purification for the soul. Then the Holy Spirit indicates that to me. He tells me so. Satan can suggest, but he cannot inspire. Hence, the necessity to discern. This discernment, which is a sheer gift of God, is given to me to see through the situation clearly.

Q. - *Can you read souls?*

A. - No. But when someone visits me, I can feel all the pain and suffering or all the joy that person is living, although I cannot see the cause. But I cannot read the state of that person's soul.

Q. - *Do you pray during these encounters with people?*

A. - Yes. While I am speaking to these people, my heart remains in a state of prayer; my soul can rise toward God while I remain attentive to the problem they are talking about.

Q. - *Can you say that you live two kinds of presence?*

A. - Yes, an invisible one, that is, the presence to the Holy Spirit. The other, visible, is the presence to the person. It is like the real Presence. I look at the host which is a visible presence at the human level and a real Presence at the supernatural level. That can be explained only through faith.

Q. - *Who are the people who come to see you most frequently?*

49

A. - All kinds of people. There are poor, wealthy, well educated, illiterate people. But often they are abandoned people who are feeling their own way and seeking God without being aware of it. There are also consecrated souls. But I especially like children. I feel at ease when talking to them about Jesus and Mary.

Q. - *Why do you like children better?*

A. - Because they are simple. They like to hear people talking about God. They always seek to know more. So when we speak of Jesus, of Mary, of the Trinity, they accept them without any discussion for they have no pride. God cannot refuse to answer their prayers. The Holy Spirit works in their hearts and makes them want to know more about Jesus and Mary. When you explain the love of God, the love of Jesus for them, they grasp this very well. They really feel they are loved and they are happy. We see there the importance of the religious education that the parents must pass on to their children at a very early age.

Q. - *Do you often receive priests?*

A. - Yes. Jesus told me to receive them with an open heart and a great deal of charity. **"Receive them through the love I put in you."**

Q. - *Whom do you see in the priests who come to you?*

A. - I see the representatives of God. But often I see them as wounded souls who need help, especially prayers. Everyday I place them in the arms of Mary, Queen of Peace, so that they may find peace of soul, heart and mind, and thus discover the faith they must have in their priesthood.

Q. - *When your visitors do not speak French, can you receive them?*

A. - Yes, for Jesus helps me. There are interpreters sometimes but if they have not rendered or translated their questions well, Jesus tells me exactly what I must understand.

Q. - *Give me an example of that.*

A. - One day, I received a Spanish-speaking lady and the interpreter had not yet arrived. When she spoke to me, Jesus made me understand her in French. When I spoke to her in French, she understood me in Spanish. When the interpreter arrived, the meeting was over and he was wondering to himself: "Why did you ask me to come?"

Q. - *Does this happen in other languages?*

A. - Yes. Jesus would help me in other languages.

Q. - *For you, Georgette, this is a particular gift!*

A. - I am always grateful to God for the gifts I receive in sheer gratuity. Encounters of this type, which He allows me to have, always bring good results because He is there to help us.

Q. - *We know, Georgette, that you do not speak any other language but French. But do you sometimes recite prayers in languages other than French?*

A. - Yes, I recite prayers in Latin like the "Pater," the "Ave Maria," and the "Gloria Patri."

Q. - *Do you sing in Latin?*

A. - Yes. Often during thanksgiving after the Holy Eucharist, I sing the "Magnificat," the "Salve Regina," and the "Ave Maria."

Q. - *Does it sometimes happen to you that you answer prayers or sing in a language unknown to you?*

A. - Yes, this has often happened for the last three years.

Q. - *Can you tell me in what language you recite or sing these prayers?*

A. - No. All I can say is that this is beyond my control. The Lord leads me to answer or to sing in another language. It is like a voice unknown to me. I hear the words within myself and in my ear. I say them or I sing them as I hear them.

Q. - *Have you ever asked the Eternal Father in what language you are praying or singing when that manifests itself?*

A. - Yes.

Q. - *Tell us how God gave you the words to an old Croatian song?*

A. - One day, I was singing the Salve Regina in Latin with the Fathers Girard. I began singing in a language I didn't know. I was hearing it sung by our Lady and that's how the song came about. Later Father Bubalo in Bosnia confirmed the song as a hymn sung in an old Croatian dialect.

Q. - *Can you say when and how the question was asked?*

A. - It was on January 24, 1986. At each celebration of the Eucharist we pray that the apparitions of the Virgin Mary at Medjugorje be recognized. So we thought it was Croatian. The question was formulated in this manner: "Most Holy Father, why do you allow your servant to pray in Croatian?"

Q. - *Did the Eternal Father give an answer?*

A. - I understood that the Eternal Father would give us an answer at the time He Himself would choose.

Q. - *Did you receive this answer?*

A. - Yes, we received it on February 26, 1986.

Q. - *What is the answer of the Eternal Father?*

A. - The Eternal Father gave me an answer which deals first with a hymn. Often this hymn rises in my heart during the act of thanksgiving. The first words are MIRTHA O MIRTHA.

Q. - *What did He say concerning this hymn?*

A. - He said: The hymn MIRTHA O MIRTHA, which can also be a recited prayer, is in Croatian.

Q. - *I would like to question you more on this*

hymn "MIRTHA O MIRTHA," but let us go back to recited prayers. Did you ask the Eternal Father what language was used in recited prayers and in spontaneous prayers?

A. - Yes, it was on Friday, the 28th of February, 1986, during the Eucharist that the Eternal Father gave me the answer.

Q. - *What is that answer?*

A. - The Eternal Father told me: **"The prayers you are reciting are in Aramaean."** And I replied to Him: **"Even the 'Hail Mary'?** And the Eternal Father answered: **"Especially the 'Hail Mary.'"**

Q. - *For what reason?*

A. - To render homage to the Queen of Peace, our Mother, Mother of the Church.

Q. - *What are the prayers most frequently recited in Aramaean?*

A. - They are the "Our Father." the "Hail Mary," the "Glory be to the Father," and the "Creed."

Q. - *When you are by yourself, do you pray also in Aramaean?*

A. - I do not know, but sometimes I pray in a strange language unknown to me.

Q. - *I would like you to recall for me what happened concerning the prayers.*

A. - Yes, I was brought a brochure in which there were prayers in Croatian. My spiritual director wanted to check without my being aware of it if I was praying in Croatian.

Q. - *Now, let us come back to the prayers. We know why the Eternal Father makes you recite the "Hail Mary" in Aramaean. You have answered that question. But, is the reason the same for the other prayers?*

A. - No, the Eternal Father told me that **"they are said in reparation for the prayers which are distorted in the Church. This is the reason why I ask you to recite these prayers in reparation for the wound made to the hearts of Jesus and Mary."**

Q. - *Did the Eternal Father give the reason for the hymn MIRTHA O MIRTHA in Croatian and the prayers in Aramaean?*

A. - Yes, and the answer is most beautiful. The hymn in Croatian renders homage to the Eternal Father through Mary. The prayers of Aramaeam render homage to Jesus and to Mary.

Q. - *Let us go back to the hymn MIRTHA O MIRTHA. On February 26, 1986, the Eternal Father said that this hymn is in Croatian. Do you sing it when you are alone by yourself?*

A. - Yes, I sometimes sing it when I am alone, but especially for the Mass and for thanksgiving. This happens more for the celebration of the Holy Eucharist and thanksgiving.

Q. - *How was this hymn given?*

A. - I hear it in my heart and in my ear. I have the words and I sing them as I hear them. But it is evident that without the help of the Virgin Mary, I would not be able to sing anything. I am but a very poor instrument which she is willing to use.

Q. - *How do you explain the help of the Virgin Mary? How do you perceive it?*

A. - When I think of my illness (oppression, angina, pulmonary infection, dizziness, etc...), my condition of extreme weakness, it is physically impossible for me to sing. So when I do so, it is the Virgin Mary who is helping me. I have not merit whatsoever for I clearly perceive that this voice which sings is totally strange to me. I perceive this voice, very soft, very young. I really am aware that Mary uses me, the poor servant that I am, to praise the Eternal Father.

Q. - *Why did the Eternal Father give you this hymn?*

A. - He gave me this hymn because it is the hymn that the Virgin Mary sings
- to magnify the Eternal Father
- and to give peace to the world.

Q. - *Has the Eternal Father said anything else about this hymn?*

A. - Yes. He said: **I offer this hymn of this prayer as a gift to the parish of Medjugorje.** He asked that the translation be made in Croatian by the author of the book *"Je vois la Vierge."* And He clearly gave the name of this priest.

Q. - *What else is there about this hymn?*

A. - The Eternal Father also said that this hymn was given out of gratitude for all the love, the respect and the fidelity of Medjugorje to and for the Queen of Peace.

Q. - *Can you sum up what happened after you received the translation of this hymn?*

A. - Yes, on February 24, 1986, we had the complete translation of the hymn MIRTHA O MIRTHA. On February 25, 1986, the Eternal Father said that the prayers are in the language of the early Church.

Q. - *How is the hymn MIRTHA O MIRTHA from the musical point of view?*

A. - On March 1, 1986, the Holy Spirit inspired the musical notation of the hymn to me.

Q. - *How was that done?*

A. - I could hear the melody, so I wrote it according to the wish of the Eternal Father. For thirty-three years I had given up music. But it was easy for me to write this because the Holy Spirit showed me the notation.

INTIMACY WITH THE ETERNAL FATHER

Q. - *Georgette, we know from the Gospel that Jesus spent long hours in prayer in the intimacy of the Eternal Father. In my conversations with you, I became aware that there was a very strong emphasis placed on the Eternal Father in the spiritual life. Could you speak more to us about this hidden treasure? But, first, since when did you begin to have this devotion?*

A. - This devotion to the Eternal Father is central to my life. But it was not so in my childhood. This devotion came later.

Q. - *Can you explain how this devotion developed?*

A. - When I was preparing to make my first communion, I began to hear the voice of Jesus. I thought it was like this for all children.

Q. - *And the voice of the Father, you could hear it?*

A. - No, this came much later.

Q. - *Did you hear the voice of the Most Blessed Virgin Mary?*

A. - Yes, when I was about 12, I could hear the voice of Mary. She made many demands from me, they were for specific intentions. She would speak to me of Jesus, His love for me and for each human being. She would speak to me of the Father and His infinite mercy. She would give me advice.

Q. - *What advice did she give you?*

A. - She would ask me to be attentive to the Holy Spirit, to pray to her in difficult moments. She would ask me to amend my shortcomings.

Q. - *What did she tell you to make you more attentive to the Holy Spirit?*

A. - She would tell me to read over often all the gifts received in Confirmation. I would reread in the catechism the parts concerning the gifts of the Holy Spirit. I tried to put them into practice. For example, during tests in school, etc...

Q. - *How did you pray to her in difficult moments?*

A. - Inwardly, I would draw nearer to her. I would take a small statue of the Blessed Virgin. I would kiss it in tears because I feared I had hurt her or Jesus.

Q. - *Why did you cry?*

A. - I was becoming more aware that my failings caused them grief. For example, if I quarreled with my brothers and sisters, I would ask Jesus and Mary to forgive me. Mary would ask me to apologize to them. She would show me very clearly how to amend my ways. When I would fall again because of my shortcomings, the Virgin Mary would suggest that I make sacrifices: go without desserts, sweets, etc... She would often urge me to be patient.

Q. - *You were telling me, a few moments ago, that your devotion to the Eternal Father developed much later. Can you tell me what was Mary's role in this devotion?*

A. - The Virgin Mary was leading me to the Eternal Father.

Q. - *In what way?*

A. - She made me accept the Father's will on many occasions, among others, accept my illness, give up music lessons because of my ill health, and also trips with my parents for the same reason. She was preparing my soul for total detachment and liberating it for prayer and quiet recollection.

Q. - *What else?*

A. - She made me understand the Father's love and mercy, for I did not know Him well. It is thanks to Mary that I understood His boundless tenderness and His infinite patience. I have always asked the Blessed Virgin to lead me to the Father as she had done with Jesus.

Q. - *Mary led you to the heart of the Eternal Father. How did He reveal Himself to you?*

A. - He revealed Himself throughHis Son, Jesus crucified. It is while contemplating the wounds of Jesus that I grasped the infinite love of the Father for each one of us, especially for the most abject, among whom I belong.

Q. - *Did you hear His voice?*

A. - Yes, but not as distinctly as I do now.

Q. - *So now, how do you hear it?*

A. - I hear the voice of the Father like a voice which reprimands me with mercy, tenderness, being all the while firm as a father's would be.

Q. - *What does the Eternal Father's voice sound like?*

A. - The Father's voice is more severe than that of Jesus. He speaks with more severity but His voice is also filled with love. His voice is like that of a father speaking to his child, teaching and correcting. Jesus' voice is softer and He pleads. It is filled with the same love as the Father but there is a recognizable difference between the two.

Q. - *What did He tell you?*

A. - As soon as He presented himself, He spoke to me of His Son. He spoke to me as a Father does to his child. Then I would address Him: "Eternal Father" or "Most Holy Father".

Q. - *How did you come to grow in the devotion to the Eternal Father?*

A. - By listening to Him attentively. I could see His great mercy in my life. And so, I began to know Him better and to serve and love Him better. This is the purpose of our existence on Earth.

Q. - *Tell us about the mercy and love of the Eternal Father?*

A. - The Eternal Father, first, is a father. He comes to us

filled with love and mercy, especially for those who suffer and those who need His mercy.

Q. - *Have you anything else to add concerning your devotion to the Eternal Father?*

A. - Yes. In fact, His love for us exceeds the love He has for His Son, because we need purification while His son gave His life to purify us. In the inmost part of His Heart as a Father, He loves us more in spite of our weaknesses and our sins. The more wretched we are, the nearer He is to us. The first step we take towards the Father, in spite of our sins, induces Him to shower us with His blessings. The least movement of repentance opens His heart to His boundless mercy, for He is always ready to receive us and to forgive us.

Q. - *Concretely how should we approach the forgiveness of the Father?*

A. - By going to Jesus, the divine Priest who gave those who represent Him the power to remit sins and, thereby, to confirm us in the forgiveness of the Father.

Q. - *What does the Eternal Father talk to you about the most?*

A. - He speaks to me of the indifference of man to His creation which is destroyed and polluted in all its aspects. Man keeps trying to discover traces of his own works throughout the universe, unable to accept God as the Creator of all that exists. He also speaks of the indifference of man towards the Church and its teachings, as well as all those who abandon the Catholic Church in search of some other understanding which will never satisfy. Paganism has filtered into the Church, into its seminaries and convents and it is one of the causes for this indifference. God also speaks of the indifference of children towards their parents and their parents toward their children. As Jesus told us; **"God the Father will vomit from His mouth those who are tepid and indifferent."**

Q. - *What does the Sacrament of Reconciliation bring to you?*

A. - The Sacrament of Reconciliation brings me a great peace of heart, of soul and of mind, because I feel the mercy of the Father, the love of Jesus and the peace of the Holy Spirit. This inner joy of the soul is given to us in the Sacrament of Reconciliation by the priest. How many depressions and anxieties would be avoided if we had recourse to this Sacrament which often heals physical (i.e., alcoholism, drugs, etc.) and moral ills. We must not forget that the Virgin Mary asks us to have recourse frequently to all the Sacraments.

Q. - *What led you to dedicate your place for prayer to the Eternal Father?*

A. - It was because of the confidences of the Eternal Father that I wanted to offer Him this sanctuary. I knew that He would be consoled by the presence of Jesus and Mary. But it is a sanctuary on earth which is not made public.

Q. - *Is there a public place dedicated to the Eternal Father?*

A. - No, the Father sadly told me one day: **'There is nowhere on earth the least chapel dedicated to my name.'**

Q. - *What was your reaction?*

A. - I was sorry and I prayed that someday there might be a public sanctuary dedicated to His Name.

Q. - *And then?*

A. - In May 1986, a chapel was dedicated to the glory of the Eternal Father. It is located in a hospital in Montreal. It was inaugurated on June 9, 1986.

Q. - *And so your wish and the will of the Father have come true?*

A. - Yes, thanks to the Lord.

HEAVEN, ANGELS, THE CELESTIAL COURT AND SATAN

Q. - *One day, you told me that you had asked the Eternal Father to send you an angel in addition to your Guardian Angel to help you in a difficult task. What did He answer?*

A. - **"Yes, because if I ask them to help you, they will obey me!"**

Q. - *Did you speak of this to your spiritual director?*

A. - Yes, and he told me: "My dear child, obey and especially do not hesitate to ask for help from the Celestial Court."

Q. - *Do you believe we each have a Guardian Angel? Even the nonbelievers?*

A. - Yes, I believe it, because we are all children of God. And God entrusts us all, believers and nonbelievers, to our Guardian Angel so that he may protect us and keep us in the love of God.

Q. - *What makes you say that?*

A. - Faith in what the Church teaches us, but also the experience of feeling that this Guardian Angel is close to me. This is difficult to describe, but it is certain that he is there. This is somewhat like a blind person being led by his guiding-dog; he does not see it, but he knows it is there. This presence is as evident as that.

Q. - *Have you seen Heaven?*

A. - Not as such. Once during a prayer vigil, I was lifted up to heaven by a vision where I saw Jesus and Mary, along with many different people who were offering gifts to the Eternal Father. I was very sad because my hands were empty. Then I saw our Heavenly Mother come near me and ask me why I was crying. I told her that my hands were empty and that I couldn't return to earth to fill them with gifts for the Eternal Father. Mary told me: **"I have a secret for you. Go and offer your heart filled with love to the Eternal Father and all will be well."** I did so after thanking her and awoke   from the vision.

Q. - *Describe the people in Heaven.*

A. - There were many people around as well as angels who were escorting Our Lady.

Q. - *You've alluded to angels. What can you tell us about angels?*

A. - I have a great devotion to angels, especially to my Guardian Angel whom I have seen on many occasions. He is dressed in white and his beauty is indescribable.

Q. - *Have you ever seen Purgatory?*

A. - No.

Q. - *Have you ever seen Hell?*

A. - No. And I wouldn't like to.

Q. - *Can you tell me what the Celestial Court has done for you?*

A. - It helps me at the spiritual level. It accompanies me in my prayer especially at the time of the Eucharist during the offering. At the moment of the consecration, it prostrates itself and adores the thrice holy God.

Q. - *Do you have more than your Guardian Angel near you?*

A. - Yes, there are angels who watch over the Alliance; there are protecting angels who shield us from Satan.

Q. - *Are there particular angels for the priests?*

A. - Yes, they have their Guardian Angel, as creatures of God. But they also have a very special angel for their priesthood, for at their consecration they are identified with Christ.

Q. - *Can you give me an example that could be verified when the Celestial Court helped you?*

A. - When the Eternal Father asked me to kneel and to prostrate myself, I had the help of the Celestial Court. I have been an invalid for thirty-two years. This was an unwise move from the human point of view, but I made it in faith to obey the Eternal Father.

Q. - *Georgette, we too often forget the angels and the celestial court, don't we?*

A. - Unfortunately, we have the tendency to forget the presence of our Guardian Angel and of the Celestial Court. Very often, the presence of our Guardian Angel is what protects us. We should invoke him and make him our confidant and our protector. It is comforting to know that he watches after us, that he sustains us in the hardships and that he will accompany us when God calls us to Himself.

Q. - *Have you anything else to add?*

A. - I advise you to have a very special devotion to Saint

Michael the Archangel, and I would like the Church to resume the recitation of the prayer of Saint Michael the Archangel after Holy Mass. This would be a good protection for all of the Church.

Q. - *Do you make a link between the Eucharist and the Celestial Court?*

A. - Yes, during the Holy Eucharist, the Eternal Father sometimes allows me to see the whole multitude of angels and saints in a state of adoration around the altar! This is an invitation to the respect and to the dignity which must be given to the celebrant and to the participants. An attitude of respect is absolutely necessary before the Real Presence. We too often forget this and we hurt the Lord by these acts of disrespect.

Q. - *Does Satan attack you when you are alone?*

A. - Yes.

Q. - *How?*

A. - He attacks me especially in my spiritual life. He persists in wanting to destroy me in my faith and in my trust. He makes me believe that all God is accomplishing in me is illusion, that I am damned for eternity. But he also attacks me when priests are here. His aggressivity is greater because they are consecrated souls. When they are here, Satan is all the more furious and he has it out on me. God allows that, for by their priesthood, they can chase him away and protect me.

Q. - *You said that Satan distorted your prayer. Can you give examples of that?*

A. - Yes. For example, he makes me say: "Thank you Jesus for allowing Satan to wander throughout the world for the good of souls" or "I hail myself Mary, Satan is with me" or again he curses the crown of thorns, the Alliance, the priests, the consecrated hands.

Q. - *Sometimes, he attacks you physically?*

A. - Yes. Sometimes, he tries to strangle me. My spiritual director has already seen for himself the imprints of his fingers on my neck. But they have always succeeded in defending me and in chasing him away from me. He dreads priesthood, especially when the priest wears his stole.

Q. - *How do these attacks end?*

A. - They stop almost every time when my spiritual director forces Satan to bow his head and recite the "Hail Mary" in full. He rages resorting to all his wiles against the title "Queen of Peace' which he invokes, but he can do nothing against Mary.

Q. - *Tell me, when did you first begin to have these attacks from Satan?*

A. - I have had them for a long time, but he is all the more furious since the Eternal Father asks me to offer Him my suffering and to pray for the authenticity of the apparitions at Medjugorje.

Q. - *Does the Devil still attack you?*

A. - I don't like to talk about him, as I've mentioned before. As for these attacks, I don't like to give any credit for them, as I believe that he can do nothing to me without God's permission. So if God permits an attack, I believe it is to put me to the test, to try my faith. God has never permitted a physical attack from Satan unless Father Guy or Armand was present. Through their priestly intervention and prayers of exorcism, the Devil is repelled and I am left with that same feeling of security I felt as I walked holding Jesus' hand.

Q. - *What does Satan look like?*

A. - I'd rather not talk about that as I would not like to influence evil spirits. I'm sorry.

Q. - *What else can you tell us about the Devil?*

A. - No. I don't like to speak of him. He is proud enough as it is, but I do want to mention that he does exist and that he is doing his best to damn the world. He infiltrates our soul through the tiniest opening that he can discover, our smallest weakness. There are many ways by which we can recognize his presence. Anything that worries us, that hurts us, that brings us anxieties and concern does not come from God but from the Evil One. Learn to say: "Get behind me Satan. You come too late. I already belong to Jesus and Mary." Many people do not believe in the existence of the Devil, passing him off as a bogey- man or and old wive's tale. It is his greatest accomplishment and its not surprising, as people do not believe in God any more, how can we expect them to believe in the Devil. One day, I asked a delivery man if he would like me to pray for him. He told me to save my energies as he didn't believe in God or the Devil and that he wasn't worth the bother. I said to him: "Whether you believe or not, one day you will come before God who created you and you will know that He does exist. I only hope you don't get to meet the other one." He said: "You're a strange lady. Can I ask you a couple of questions?" We sat down and spoke for about an hour. When he left he thanked me for presenting God to him in such a loving and informative way. That is one of our greatest flaws about the loving God who created us and before whom we will all stand in judgement one day.

Q. - *What can you tell us concerning the Triumph of the Immaculate Heart of Mary?*

A. - I pray for it with all my heart, because in that Triumph we will witness the Triumph of Jesus and of God the Father. I ask all souls to pray for that day of Triumph.

Q. - *What do you know about the conversion of Russia?*

A. - I rely on what was asked of us in Fatima and the certainty that if we are united to her though the Rosary, Russia will be converted.

Q. - *What can you tell us about Mary as Co-Redemptrix, Mediatrix and Advocate?*

A. - I ask God the Father that everything be done in

accordance to His Holy Will. It is God the Father who will decide by placing in the hearts of men His Great Plan of Love and His wish for all to recognize Mary as Co-Redemptrix, Mediatrix of all Graces and Advocate.

SPIRITUAL SURVIVAL
IN A TROUBLED WORLD

Q. - *Father Guy said that in order to prevent an abortion, you once experienced the pregnancy of a woman. Can you tell us about that?*

A. - A woman who lived next door to me had two children, eighteen and sixteen years of age. When she became pregnant, she decided to have an abortion as she didn't want another child. Our Lady came to me and asked me to pray for this woman which I did. The next day, the Lord asked me if I would be willing to carry this child and I agreed, not knowing what it would be like. My stomach began to swell, I had morning nausea and my breasts ached. One morning, my milkman said: "I'm sorry! I've always called you Miss Faniel. I didn't know you were married." The mother finally gave birth to a healthy little girl and I am her God-mother. I've lived two other such spiritual pregnancies. These pregnancies were carefully monitored by my doctor.

Q. - *Has the Eternal Father spoken to you about the world? How bad the world has become?*

A. - First of all, sin is an offense against God. Our Eternal

Father gives us all the graces we need in order to avoid sin, to overcome our weaknesses, our tendencies. He gave us the Sacrament of confession to cleanse us and heal us when we fall. He invites us to the Eucharist, that He might fortify us against those same weaknesses. Even now, Our Lord's Heart is wounded by our indifference, our ingratitude and our sins. Our values and our priorities are all mixed up. Not so long ago, our priorities were: God, the Church, our family, our work, our friends, comforts and finally entertainment. We don't have that vision any longer. Pleasure, money entertainment seem to come first and God comes last. We must be aware of all that God does for us every day. Human beings today are convinced that they are due everything, that they are enlightened to everything, no matter that one's neighbor might be starving before our eyes.

Q. - *What does sin do to us?*

A. - Sin destroys us by separating us from God. It separates us from charity, the love and the mercy which God Almighty would like to bestow upon us. If after spending a lifetime nurturing, raising and loving your children, one of these children were to say to you: "You've never loved me. You've never done anything for me," wouldn't you be devastated?

Q. - *Has the Holy Trinity ever spoken to you about the Chastisement? The Great Tribulation? The Warning? The Miracle? The Era of Peace?*

A. - No. I've read about these subjects but have had no personal revelation concerning them.

Q. - *What has God taught you about the Eucharist in helping us during these trying times?*

A. - God has taught me how the Eucharist contains not only Jesus and the Son but also the Father and the Holy Spirit. The angels in heaven kneel and adore the Holy Eucharist. How many of us receive communion quickly and run off to our daily preoccupations without adoring the very presence of God in our soul. And so the angels adore the divine majesty in the Eucharist. The Eucharist fortifies us and helps us to accept the weaknesses in those around us, to love all aspects of our life, including setbacks, injuries and death. God does not lack in generosity.

Q. - *About Reconciliation?*

A. - Reconciliation is part of charity. God's first commandment is to love our God and to love our neighbor as ourselves. If there was reconciliation between men, between government leaders, between Church leaders, the world would be filled with love and charity and would thus know true peace. To many people these days, peace consists in not being disturbed or bothered, doing as they please. In order to have peace, we must have reconciliation. Criticism is much easier than understanding and acceptance. Some of us don't like a certain priest or a certain bishop. Others don't like our Pope. Criticism is easy and as such it renders reconciliation difficult. We are all God's children and we must be reconciled with one another if we want to be reconciled with God.

Q. - *About Penance?*

A. - As for penance, God grants us so many opportunities each and every day to do penance for our faults. The Gospels are full of examples. That is why it is so important for us to read the Bible everyday, especially the Gospel reading for the day and to try to live its message in our life. If everyone did this, we would only have saints in the world. There are so many ways by which we can do Penance, depriving ourselves of those little things we enjoy so much. We can observe the visionaries of Medjugorje to learn how to fast or do penance.

Q. - *About conversion?*

A. - Conversion must come from within. People say: "I forgive, but." True conversion implies completely forgiving those who hurt us. We need to ask God to grant us that charity because it doesn't come naturally.

Q. - *Has God talked to you about prayer?*

A. - Jesus Himself taught us to pray the "Our Father." If we pray the "Our Father" with faith and apply in our life everything that prayer teaches us and which unites all the souls in the universe until the ends of time, we would change the world. Prayer of the heart is very easy to do. It is the intimacy between our soul and God. We need to speak to our Heavenly Father as would a child who is suffering and who seeks solace and comfort from a parent. There are no secrets with God. He knows and sees all. We should hold nothing back from Him, secure in the knowledge that He will always hear our prayer. Sometimes a person tells me that God doesn't listen to his or her prayers. I tell that person, "You are wrong. You judge God severely. God answers all our prayers, but in His time, which is not our time." If our Eternal Father did not answer our prayers, He would act contrary to what Jesus taught us: **"Ask and it shall be given. Knock and the door will be opened."** God cannot refuse to ignore His Son's teachings. That is why God sent Jesus to earth, to teach us how to love and how to pray. Prayer doesn't have to be complicated. Invoke the Holy Spirit and ask Him to help you formulate your prayer to the Father.

Q. - *How often and how much do you pray?*

A. - I have no given hours. I often pray late into the night or awake in the middle of the night to pray. I am usually up by six and pray for an hour before I receive communion. Prayer is a really an elevation of our heart and soul to God in a communion of love and spirit. As such, I offer every heartbeat to the Eternal Father in love and thanksgiving. I offer up to God all the sorrows and sufferings that are not offered, either by unconsciousness by ignorance or by non-belief.

Q. - *What are your favorite verses of Scripture?*

A. - The Passion. I feel drawn by the passage, especially during lent. I unite my whole being to Christ, in my physical and moral suffering. Jesus is so good to me, allowing me to participate in His Passion and death.

Q. - *What else can you tell us about the Celestial Court?*

A. - The Celestial Court helps me greatly when I am experiencing a lot of difficulty. The Eternal Father taught me how to implore the help of the Celestial Court. At that time, I was working a lot with immigrants, preparing care packages and I couldn't tie the cords around the packages as my hands caused me to suffer so. I asked the Eternal Father to send my Guardian-Angel to help me. God the Father told me to ask for the Celestial Court to help me. I was so surprised! I said: "Me?" He said: "**Yes. If you obey Me, the angels obey me.**" I have asked them to help me on many occasions, especially when I am in need of consolation. Everyday, I pray the Celestial Court to go throughout the world, protecting the children of God from the Evil One who is seeking to destroy God's creation.

Q. - *What can you tell us about intercession?*

A. - You have to have faith in the one you are involving. In my case, it's our Eternal Father. I don't pray for myself as such, but I pray for all souls that not one soul be lost because I didn't pray for it, to pray that no sin be committed because no one interceded for that soul. I offer prayers on intercession for those who do not offer their sufferings, either because they do not believe or because they are not in a condition to offer them. I pray prayers of intercession for those who hunger, for those who are without work, for priests and nuns who are confused or tormented and who hesitate in their mission. These souls chosen by God to shepherd His flock, need an emotional

balance in their religious life. I pray for
missionaries and for government leaders. I pray
for teenagers, for married couples that are breaking
up. Prayers of intercession are constantly present in
my life. I beg God to forgive all those who neglect
Him. I plead that He receive in Heaven, all those
children given to Mary at the foot of the Cross.
That is my deepest prayer of intercession.

Q. - *Mary's intercession?*

A. - Mary prays to our Heavenly Father constantly,
interceding for us, imploring God to grant us all the
graces we need in order to remain faithful to His
will. Mary has accepted time and time again to visit
us here on earth, teaching us and calling us back to
her Son Jesus. Our Lady's' intercessions are precious
to the Father. We need to heed her messages and to
do our best to live these messages every moment of
our life. How many times has she intervened in our
life to protect us from harm without our being aware
of it, even before the intervention of our Guardian-
Angel? I am convinced that Mary holds the innocent
victims of abortion close to her heart, just as she held
the Child-Jesus. They are martyrs in every sense of
the word. Our Lady's sorrow over these children is
immense, especially when we consider her maternal
instinct. She knows how much all her children need
her love, protection and guidance.

Q. - *What can you tell us about Saints?*

A. - There are so many. I don't know them all. I
consider St. Theresa as a little sister who was
given to us by God as a rose among us. Then

there is St. Joseph who has played a major role in my life. We are witnesses to his intervention in our life through the many miracles which have occurred at the Oratory in Montreal. I read somewhere that if we pray that Saint who's feast day it is, he will greet us personally when we got to Heaven.

Q. - *Has God talked to you about the future?*

A. - No. But He asks me to pray constantly for world peace.

Q. - *Do you have any prophecies from Mary, Jesus or the Eternal Father?*

A. - Not as such. By rereading my spiritual notes, Fathers Guy and Armand have recognized some events of which I had written in the past. But I receive no prophecies as such.

Q. - *What do you pray for now?*

A. - I also pray for the authentification of the apparitions in Medjugorje. I pray for the visionaries, that they not become spiritually proud through their mission.

Q. - *Have you had any special visions you can tell us about?*

A. - One day, I received permission from my doctor to go to church where the Blessed Sacrament was displayed for 40 hours. I searched the shelve of my bookcase, trying to find a book that I could bring and which would help me to spend an hour before the Blessed Sacrament. I couldn't find any. But the Lord said to me: **"Just come and spend some time with me   and open your heart to My Presence."** When I bowed before Him in the Blessed Sacrament, I was suddenly filled with a deep feeling of peace. Then I saw Jesus standing by my side. He took my hand and we began walking on a very long, narrow and winding road. I heard soft music playing. I remember the feeling of security I felt as I walked with Jesus. After the vision ended, I sat before the Blessed Sacrament and the Lord spoke to me. He helped me to understand how long   and difficult the road to His Father's Kingdom can be. I understood how the only way I could travel it without harm is by walking hand in hand with Jesus and looking in front of me. Jesus said: **"Do not look to the left or to the right, as there are cliffs and precipices on both sides."**

Q. - *Has God spoken to you about the Pope?*

A. - Yes, He asked me on many occasions to pray for the Pope and for the spiritual renewal of the Church.

Q. - *Will there be a false pope?*

A. - I've read books that speak of the antichrist, but I don't know much about these matters. When Pope John Paul II was elected, especially after the short reign of John Paul I, many said that this Pope would be with us for along time, as he was young, energetic and very athletic. But Our Lady told me: "The Cross my Pope will have to carry will make an old man of him prematurely." That was on his election day. I asked the Lord: "Who will be our Pope?" The Lord said: **"He is the fruit of My Father's will. Like Me, he will have a deep love in his heart for the poor and suffering of the world. He will be a mediator between God and man. Like Me, he will suffer much and he will give his life for his flock."**

Q. - *Has God talked to you about the Catholic Church?*

A. - The greatest attack upon the Church today is an indirect attack. We hear of the infiltration of evil men in the Church hierarchy, but the Church's greatest enemy is our indifference to Her. Many don't care about Her teachings or if they know them, ignore them completely, picking and choosing what is convenient. Who is really to blame? Can we blame the clergy for not teaching black from white, leaving gray areas to be interpreted as we see fit? That would not be fair because not all are tepid in their faith. No we are all to blame, especially those of us who are aware of this spiritual attack because we do not pray and fast for the Church and so we allow weaknesses to grow and become festered.

Q. - *Thank you and God Bless you, Georgette.*

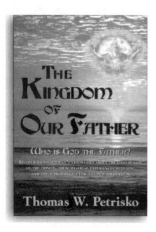
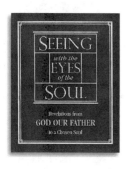

82

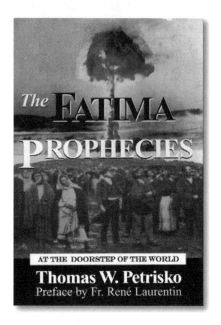